THE ABUSED QUEEN

Praise for *The Abused Queen*

In *"The Abused Queen"*, you find yourself with the rare opportunity to walk in another woman's shoes. Many who have never endured the stigma or pain of domestic abuse will learn almost firsthand how it played out in this author's life. Stella Kiinama bares her soul with cringe-worthy details, without letting it break her spirit. Even though the pain and despair are real, so is the hope and healing. Victory is seen in more ways than just surviving the abuse; it is also evident in how she allowed the peace of God to guide her into a bright and fearless future.

Jacqui Hill Goudeau
Author of *A Shoppers Guide to Dating*,
Speaker, Life Renovator

This is a book that brings to light the grim truth and reality of most people's life. Stella has done an excellent job showing in graphic detail how easy it is to be a predator's prey when you don't understand your purpose in life. The lessons learnt are invaluable to both men and women who want to live an enriching and meaningful life.

Dr. Charles Kinuthia
Certified Business Coach,
International Speaker, Trainer
Author of *Unlimited Possibilities*

Stella's captivating story is one you will never forget. In her book, *The Abused Queen*, she recounts her horrific encounter with her abuser, and she offers an authentic firsthand experience, as well as solutions she learned the hard way, for everyone going through any type of abuse in marriage. I have had the privilege to mentor and impact Stella and have seen her develop into an agent of transformation and change. She relentlessly pursues informing, equipping, inspiring, and impacting other women with her story. Stella has something to say, and we all need to listen as she unveils an issue she has personally experienced, but an issue very few are willing to talk about.

Dr. Phinehas Kinuthia
Senior Pastor Faith City Church
Author of *Dreaming to Becoming*

An individual's experience of trauma and pain is a very personal thing. All emotions, even those that are suppressed and unexpressed, have physical effects. Unexpressed emotions are poisonous to the entirety of oneself. Stella chose to be naked before the world not only to heal herself but heal many others, male and female alike. This is an inspirational journey of emotional strength and spiritual growth. I have mentored this beautiful spiritual daughter, and I have observed the fruit of forgiveness and spiritual maturity.

Rev. Ruth Ngigi
Kingdom Mysteries International

THE ABUSED QUEEN

A True Story about Escaping the firm Grip of Abuse

STELLA KIINAMA

I have tried to recreate events, locales, and conversations from my memories of them. In order to maintain others' anonymity, in some instances I have changed the names of individuals and places, and I may have changed some identifying characteristics and details such as physical properties, occupations, and places of residence.

Nelson Mandela quote is found at www.goodread.com.

Photo Cover by Trevoy Kelly, www.trevoykellyphotography.com

Cover design by Camille Rejenne Pavon

ISBN 9781987674934

DEDICATION

To my daughter, Charlene, this journey called life might be bumpy at times, but never forget that God's got your back, and His love for you is infinite!

CONTENTS

ACKNOWLEDGMENTS

To God. Lord, you have been the only solid being in my life. Looking back, I see how you carried me, made ways where I didn't see any, closed some wrong doors, and kept me from all kinds of danger, including death. May glory and honor forever be yours from the deepest part of my soul.

To my mom, Florence Wanjiku Kiinama. You are truly one in six billion. If I had to choose how I would re-enter this world, I would choose you all over again. You have been everything I could ever ask for in a parent. You have loved me, guided me, believed in me, and, most important, prayed for me since I was a baby. You still do. May the good Lord keep you in perfect health and increase the length of your days. I love you more than words could ever express. Thank you also for the team you and Dad put together—my brothers and sisters, who have been the best characters in this movie called life. I cherish you all.

My lovely daughter, Charlene Shiku. You are the love of my life. You are the apple of my eye. I know God loves me because He trusted you with me. You are the perfect gift, more than I ever hoped for. I sometimes wonder what life was about before you showed up. I pray that you will forever know your value. Keep your loving nature, for it will heal many.

To my friends who have stuck with me and believed in me even when the bottom fell out. Ruth M. Ngaari, Peter Gichuhi, George G. Kamau, Chrispus M, and countless others. Thank you for your encouraging words and always wanting the best for me.

Salome Gichui. You are more than a friend. You are an angel and a destiny connector. This work would not have been possible without the countless hours you put in praying for and encouraging me. I truly appreciate you. May God see you through your endeavors.

To my spiritual parents, Pastor Dr. Phinehas Kinuthia and First Lady Joyce Kinuthia. Thank you for the transformation you have made in my spiritual life. I am blessed to have you as my shepherds.

To my coach, Dr. Charles Kinuthia (CK factor). Thank you for discovering me, believing in me and my dreams, and for the efforts you have put into changing the structure of my life. Because of you, I developed enough courage to put my experience into writing, hoping to help many. May God continue to enlarge your territory.

INTRODUCTION

I am indeed a living testimony, a manifestation of the saving power of God. I'm encouraged by the words of Prophet Isaiah: "When you go through deep waters, I will be with you. When you go through rivers of difficulty, you will not drown. When you walk through the fire of oppression, you will not be burned up; the flames will not consume you" (43:2: NLT).

I was in real deep waters for the five years I was married to Rex. But God in His faithfulness did not let me drown, and when the fire was applied, even though I was burnt, it did not consume me. The only thing that was consumed were the ropes that had bound me in a dysfunctional marriage. God is true to His Word!

I believe God saved me from that abusive marriage for a reason. One reason is to allow me to share my story of abuse in the hopes of saving others the pain and sorrow I experienced. By writing this book, I desire to share the lessons and tools I gained through my abuse. Equally important, I hope to demonstrate that the love I desired and looked for in the wrong places I found only in God, who loved me enough send His only Son, Jesus, to die for my sins. In Jesus, I found not only my purpose but also my value and self-worth.

To those of you have who have gone through, are going through, or might go through abuse, please know that there is life after abuse.

The two main reasons I chose to write this book are: Domestic violence is on the rise. The statistics for 2013 state that in one minute, 24 people are abused either physically, sexually or by stalking in United states of America alone. There are so many unsuspected abusers out there and even more unsuspecting victims.

According to the Centers of Disease Control statistics of July 2017, half of all female homicides are killed by intimate partners. These numbers are alarming to me and they should be to all of us. Does it mean that the measures and interventions that are already in place are not working or where are we going wrong? In my opinion, this calls for desperate measures. What has worked so far, what is not working and what can we add.

The other reason was because we sometimes find ourselves making poor or wrong choices in relationships and marriages. Its not surprising to find ourselves in an abusive or toxic relationship. That was exactly the spot I found myself in. I wasn't sure if I would make it out alive or I would die trying to get out. At that very critical moment, I cried onto my God to rescue me. And He did.

The bible says He is not a respecter of people, that means if He heard my prayer and answered it, He will rescue you if you call on Him! Try it!

CHAPTER 1

HAPPY BEGINNING

Born into a family of eight children, I enjoyed a fun-filled childhood. I am the fifth-born child, between two boys; therefore, being a tomboy was inevitable. My older brother was five years older than I, so we didn't share a close relationship or do much together. He considered me a baby. My younger brother and sister, however, were my partners in all manner of crime.

My family looked like two sets of people. There were the older kids and the younger kids. I was the oldest of the younger kids. Before me were two brothers and two sisters.

Ours was a very humble upbringing. My mom was the only breadwinner, and she had no regular income. The struggles were real, but through her strong faith in God, she managed to provide food and school fees while making a home for us. Poverty didn't keep us down. My mom did her best to raise all eight of us by herself. I will always honor her for giving up her needs to make sure we kids were well taken care of.

In the evenings, we sat around the fire, laughing explosively at the stories our older brother told. He was quite a comedian. I believe it's fitting to say that I had a good childhood, and for that I am grateful.

One day when I was in high school, we were on the farm with my mom. As we were talking, she told me that she'd been married to a different man before my dad. The man was the father of my first four siblings. The marriage failed because her ex-husband was abusive. He would come home from work drunk, and the smallest disagreement seemed to ignite an argument, which would, in most cases, end up in him beating her, even threatening to kill her and her kids someday.

She'd endured the abuse because it was normal back then for husbands to beat their wives. But the situation changed once he started beating on the kids. At one point he hit my oldest brother in the forehead with a metal can because he wasn't eating his dinner fast enough. Blood gushed from his wound, and he had to be rushed to the hospital. The kids were terrified of their father. Then one day he came home drunk and, as usual, started a fight. This day, though, he took an axe and started slashing the furniture and hacking walls in the house, swearing to kill everyone. He chopped the coffee table and a couple of chairs into pieces before he finally paused.

My terrified mother was curled up in one corner, holding on to her kids and praying for God to save them. A little later, he stepped out to get more alcohol and promised to kill them all once he returned. Mom grabbed the opportunity, gathered her four young kids, and ran away, with nothing but the clothes on their backs. She told us how that day she had made up her mind never to go back to him, no matter what. She worked different manual jobs to fend for her young family. It was very hard. Then four years later, she met my father, whom she soon married.

Hearing her story was like watching a horror movie. I couldn't imagine going through such a terrifying experience. I was sorry that my own mother had to suffer through such a horrific situation. But most important, I was glad that she chose to leave the man.

My biological father died when I was ten years old, after a long struggle with asthma. He was the coolest dad for the few years I was blessed to know him. I never saw him get physical with mum or argue in our presence. I'm sure they had their issues and disagreements, but that they didn't show them to us made my dad my hero and he will remain so forever.

My mom couldn't afford to send me to college right out of high school. My younger brother and sister were still in high school, and she could barely afford to take care of their school expenses. I decided to go to Nairobi, Kenya's capital city, and try to make a life for myself. Mom would not let me go without a fight, because she believed I was too young at the age of twenty to leave home and find my way in a big city. But I was determined, and with the help of my big sister, I escaped from home, hoping that one day my mom would forgive me and be proud of me.

Deep inside, I believed God was with me and wanted me to try out life. After a few years of struggling in Nairobi, I landed a sales and marketing job. Two years later, I was able to start my own marketing firm. Life was starting to make sense. By then, I had made peace with my mother and acquired her blessings.

In 2008, by divine intervention, I was selected among many to live, work, and study in the United States of America. That was beyond electrifying. I was totally blown away by the offer. Growing up, I had imagined America to be one step away from heaven. In my mind, going to America was only for the rich and famous. The chance to do something like this was too huge for me to comprehend. But somehow, God had made a way, and I was willing to grab this opportunity and walk this path. Off to United States of America I flew. Little did I know what was waiting for me on the other side of the Atlantic Ocean!

CHAPTER 2

FIRST ENCOUNTER

I landed in Birmingham, Alabama. Life in America started well. Then culture shock set in. I was lucky to have had very gracious hosts, who taught me the dos and don'ts of the new land. I quickly realized that USA was very different from my homeland.

For instance, in Kenya a personal car was a luxury. Most people took public transportation to and from work, but in America, a car was as necessary as a place to live, if not more. I also needed official paperwork, like a Social Security Card and a driver's license to even apply for a job. These were unheard of back in Kenya. It took a while to acquire the documents and then to find work.

The only person I knew in this country was Jay, also a Kenyan. My boss back home had introduced us a couple years prior. Jay had been in America for a while at this point, and for about a year we communicated through emails and phone calls. I fell for him—hard. But when he found a girlfriend in America, he quit calling and writing. Even at this, he and his roommates let me live with them in America until I could get myself established.

One day a new friend and I stopped in a grocery store. It was there that I met Rex. Later that day he called the friend I was with and asked for my phone number. Sometime later, he called me, but I could not recall meeting him. He explained how I had met him at the store where he worked. Then he offered to give me a ride if I ever needed one. I thanked him, hung up, and put him out of my mind.

I didn't think twice about him, for I was focused on getting a stable job, a car, and place to live. My goals were set. Even at that, I didn't mind having him as a friend, but I was too busy building my life in America to even consider any serious relationships.

About three months after my arrival to the States, I wanted out of Jay's apartment. Though we had broken up before I had ever arrived in America, I still had feelings for him. Staying with him was made even more difficult by his girlfriend's regular visits. Each time she came by felt like I was being stabbed in the chest. I needed to get out of this place where my feelings were being hurt every day and no one seemed to notice.

Through a friend of his, I found a lady who needed a roommate. I still had not landed a job, but she allowed me to move in while I continued to look for a job. I was more than ready to move out of Jay's place. I didn't have much to carry, just two suitcases of clothes. Whew! Finally, my misery was over.

My new roommate, a beautiful Kenyan lady, was nice to me from the first meeting. She showed me around the apartment. We agreed on what bills we could share as soon as I got a job. Everything sounded acceptable.

On the second night at her place, her ex-boyfriend came by. I introduced myself to him, and we all spent a big part of that night chatting and watching TV. I was starting to feel at home.

Eventually, I attained the necessary documents and found my first job at Olive Garden, which proved to be the hardest job I've ever done. With my British English, I could not pronounce the names of the foods on the menu. This frustrated not only myself and my boss but also my customers. I was not on salary, so tips were the only money I got to take home. I would get $2 and at most $10 a day. I soon realized that my dream to become a millionaire was farfetched while working at Olive Garden.

A little later, I got a job as a cashier at a Walmart Supercenter. That job was much easier, even though it was still challenging for customers to understand me. They complained that my accent was too thick. Sometimes, when they asked a question, I didn't know the answer to, I'd page the manager to answer them. A few people thought my ignorance was funny, but others were annoyed and muttered unkind remarks, which, in time, I learned to ignore.

I worked the 2 p.m. to 10 p.m. shift. Still without a car, I had to depend on the goodwill of my few friends for rides. Since my shift started in the middle of the day, it was difficult to find anyone who was free at that time. Luckily, my roommates' ex's shift ended at 1 p.m., and he was always available to drop me off to work and sometimes pick me up.

After four months, I still had not saved enough money to buy a car. I depended mostly on the kindness of others who gave me rides to and from work. One day, I was stranded at the house. I had thirty minutes to get to work and couldn't find anyone to give me a ride. It was then I remembered Rex and his offer.

I called and asked for help, which he willingly obliged. During the ride to work, I got to know a little about him. When we arrived, he asked if I would go out with him sometime. Until this time, he was the only guy I had met who wasn't married or in a serious relationship. He wasn't bad looking and seemed quite funny. I thought about it for about three seconds then said yes. I walked into my workplace excited about my new friend.

Even though the idea of going out with a guy sounded good, I was not looking for a relationship, and marriage was not anywhere in my mind. By then, I'd had my own share of relationship issues within the first few months in the "Promised Land." So, I had decided to lay low for a while and focus on my goals.

It wasn't long before by roommate's ex told me he was interested in me and wanted us to date.

"I appreciate your kindness, but since you are my roommate's ex, I cannot date you."

But he didn't stop asking. He blamed my roommate for ordering me not to date him. When she learned of this, she was furious at the false accusation. She surprised me when she said, "Please date him. I owe him a lot, and if you date him, he won't be upset with me."

"What do you owe him?" I asked.

"It's too complicated to go into. Just date him."

"Look, I'm not going to date your ex. It just doesn't seem right. Besides, I'm not looking for a relationship at this time."

I remember that day like it was yesterday.

About a week and a half later, all hell broke loose one night when I was in his car. He was taking me home from work when I received a text from my roommate. "I left the house key under the mat outside the door, please pack all your belongings and get out of my house. Make sure you put the key back under the mat before you leave!"

Hot tears rolled down my cheeks. "Oh, my goodness!" What was happening? Why? Go where?

Realizing my distress, he asked what was wrong. I handed him the phone. He tried to call her after reading the text, but she didn't pick up. I felt totally lost.

After consoling me, he took me to pick up my clothes. Then we went to the Purple Onion restaurant in Homewood, where he bought me dinner. I couldn't eat anything. My head was throbbing with questions and concerns. Without any warning, I was homeless and carless. I had a minimum-wage job. How could I support myself? How was I going to make it? I contemplated returning to Kenya, but I had emptied my bank accounts and sold my business before I left for the States.

"Just leave me here and I'll figure out what to do next," I said.

"I am not leaving you here. There's a vacant room in the three-bedroom house I share with my cousin. I'm sure she won't mind your staying there until you're stable enough to make it on your own."

I still thank God for him to this day. He was very helpful and respectful to me.

I was torn into pieces when I later learned that my name was being dragged throughout the Kenyan community in Birmingham. I was labeled "boyfriend snatcher." Not just by my former roommate but also by Jay's girlfriend! How could I argue with them? How could I fight them? How could I convince people that this was a lie and I was not interested in anyone's boyfriend?

I realized then that it takes only one or two people with an evil heart and a big mouth to ruin your reputation. Every day rumors smear and defame the characters of many innocent people. I chose silence as the best answer to the false allegation. I ignored the gossip and kept on living. I remained there for four months.

I got a better-paying job at a rehabilitation center, bought a used car, and moved into a two-bedroom apartment with a female friend and workmate in Homewood, Alabama.

After all that drama, I was afraid to even talk to a man, especially a Kenyan. But when I confirmed that Rex was truly single, I was fine with having him as a friend. After all, he seemed to understand and see my innocence.

Rex and I eventually went out for our first date: dinner and a movie. I liked that he shared my love of watching movies. We had lots of laughs when we were together. I enjoyed being with him. As far as I was concerned, we were just casual friends.

One day, he asked me to go out of state for a weekend with him and a couple of his friends. I was thrilled by the offer. At last I would get to see some other parts of America.

The weekend came that we were to leave. Rex picked me up at my apartment. The road-trip to charlotte North Carolina was fun. We had a chance to ride a boat on lake Wylie, enjoyed the beautiful Daniel Stowe botanical gardens and did much more.

When Rex brought me back home and we turned the corner to my apartment block, we were shocked to find the building wrapped in bright yellow tape with the words "Police Line Do Not Cross."

CHAPTER 3

COMMON LAW MARRIAGE

"Come We Stay" Arrangement

One of the apartments on my block had caught fire, and even though the firefighters had come on time to keep the damage to a minimum, the AC system needed to be replaced for the whole block. The leasing office said it would take approximately two weeks to install a new one. No one was allowed in until the new system was installed. I was lost, not knowing where I'd go for the next two weeks. As I was trying to come up with a plan, I decided to call a girlfriend from my village I had just met. But before I could call her, Rex suggested I stay with him while I waited. I knew it was a bad idea since I didn't know him well, but I agreed because I felt like saying no would hurt his feelings, especially after his giving me such a fun weekend.

So, I agreed to his offer. We picked up a few of my belongings and off we went to his apartment. I was happy he volunteered, but I also knew for two weeks that I would be a "temporary wife." But what better way to get to know him better than staying with him? At least, this is how I convinced myself.

The guy clearly showed me that he loved and cared for me. He complimented me and literally worshipped everything I did and was. He would go on and on about my beauty, how proud he was for winning a "jackpot." He praised my cooking and cleaning skills. His attention and affirmation felt good, like a balloon full of helium sailing in the air. With that kind of validation, it wasn't hard to fall for him.

He worked two jobs and had only Sundays off. I loved that he worked hard and was not a party person. When he was off work, we talked a lot. I learn about his childhood and upbringing, as he learned about mine. He did some things in his adolescence years that were as serious as committing minor crimes. "I was young and stupid. But that was then and I know better now."

I thought about how we have all done irresponsible things in our early years that we are not proud of today, and so I overlooked his misdeeds. Looking back, I should have run. But on the surface, everything seemed to be going so well.

I called my leasing office two weeks later to check on the status of moving back in. I was greatly disappointed to learn that the apartment wasn't ready yet. When I told Rex this, he looked straight into my eyes and said, "Why don't we get married?"

Get married? I was surprised by the quick decision. I wasn't ready for it. I was fine with having a boyfriend to talk to and do things with, like other big girls and boys. My gut screamed NO! I was about to break my own rule of avoiding anything serious other than focusing on my goals. Another part of me said that he seemed like a good guy. What if I walked away from him and someone else stepped in? My mind was shooting questions to my spirit, which insisted on saying no. I knew it was not right, but where could I go from here? Who would take me in after all the gossip that had gone around?

Then I learned that my roommate had decided to marry her longtime boyfriend, which meant I didn't have a roommate and couldn't afford the rent by myself.

Rex's idea sounded like a good idea at the time. I said yes to his "proposal." He gave me a secondhand ring. I was on cloud nine.

Looking back now, I see that I acted really desperate to accept something that was below what I believed I deserved.

Soon after we started living together, Rex's dad took ill and died shortly after. This loss broke Rex. I did my best to comfort and stand by him. I mourned with him, and after a few months of grieving, he started to heal from the loss.

About six months after we started living together, I asked Rex, "What is next for our relationship?" I wanted to know if he was serious about marriage, or if he was just looking for some fun.

CHAPTER 4

THE UNFORESEEABLE

In our African culture, particularly in Kenya, one must follow several steps regarding marriage. The couple-to-be must inform their respective families of their desire to marry. The groom's family is required to go to the bride's family and announce their son's interest in their daughter. They bring with them a monetary gift. This step equates to engagement. It means that the bride-to-be and her family cannot receive or entertain any other suitors unless the two lovers indicate otherwise.

Rex had promised to call his mom and let her know about me and our plans. A couple of weeks later, I questioned Rex.

"What did your mom say about us?"

He looked at me startled, even fearful. He hadn't called her, and I guess he realized I took the tradition seriously. So, he picked up his cell phone and called his mother. He put the phone on speaker phone, and I was able to listen in on their conversation.

The usual conversation between mother and son went on for a while, and then he told her that he wanted to share some good news with her. "You remember Stella?"

"Yes, I remember her," she replied.

Rex went on to tell her that I was really a nice girl and he was considering marrying me. There was a long pause on the other end of the phone. "Mom, are you still there?"

"Yes. I didn't expect such news."

I heard disappointment in her voice. This was not good news to her at all. Oblivious of the fact that I was listening, she started by which part of Kenya I came from.

He answered.

After another long pause, she said, "Why don't you wait till we finish the building project we were working on first? Why the rush? You know girls from that area only spend your money or get you to send it to their own families!"

Words cannot express the bewilderment that settled over me. I could not believe she had made such a cruel accusation. My knees became weak. My legs gave out as I lowered myself down onto the chair. I gasped for air.

Rex tried to stop her from talking anymore, but she kept going, discouraging him and attempting to talk him out of the idea of marriage.

I could not believe my ears. Although I had never met this woman in person, all she had heard about me was positive and that I was nice and helpful to Rex. And yet she didn't think I was the right fit for her son. No words can explain the level of pain I felt.

Seeing how bothered I was, Rex disconnected the phone, promising to call his mother back later. He wrapped me in a hug and held me close. "I'm so sorry, Stella. Mom is just being protective of me and is still overwhelmed by the loss of Dad. Now she feels like she's about to lose her son, too."

His words did little to comfort me. I was hurt, and I felt the sting of rejection deep in my heart.

That was the perfect reason to leave the relationship right then, but I didn't get the very big hint or see the red flag. I hoped that one day, once she got a chance to meet me, she would totally love me, just like her son did.

What I know now is, it's better to go where you are celebrated than where you are tolerated. Besides, man's rejection is often God's protection.

CHAPTER 5

NEGOTIATIONS

Eventually, Rex convinced his mother that I was a hardworking lady, and together we could finish up the building project they were working on much faster. She reluctantly agreed for us to marry. At this point, my mom knew very little about the relationship except that I was seeing someone. She certainly had no idea I was living with a man.

Honestly, I had doubts about it being a good idea to continue with the marriage. Everything in me told me to run away as fast as I could. But that would come with a lot of explaining to my friends and workmates. I had already bragged to them about Rex being a good guy and I was about to get married. Most of them had encountered resistance from future mother in-laws, and so I let them convince me that Rex's mom's attitude toward me was not a big deal or enough reason to leave.

Eventually, I mentioned to my mother that I was considering getting married. Even though she was worried that I hadn't known the guy long enough, she seemed thrilled, especially because at twenty-eight years of age, I had not introduced any prospective son-in-law to her. I had decided that she would meet only the man who would become my husband. I told her all the good stuff about Rex and his family, avoiding giving too many details. Telling her what was really going on would yield different results than I wanted. Looking back, that was a big mistake because a mother always wants the best for her daughter. I'm sure she would have advised me on the best route to take. But I was still hopeful that the situation with my prospective mother in law would improve.

The time came when the two families were supposed to meet. The groom's family usually gives a date to the bride's family, who then prepares to receive them. Both families have representatives, usually elderly men, to speak on behalf of each family.

During this time, Rex had lost his full-time job and had only a part-time job, where he worked three days a week, earning very little money. I, on the other hand, was in school full time in the morning and worked full time as a Certified Nurse Assistant in the evenings. Not much money for that position either, but I wasn't going to let anything go wrong during this important occasion. I wanted to make a good impression on my family.

I worked hard, picking up extra shifts at work. I sent some money to my mom so she could do some fix-ups to ensure that our home looked presentable on the material day. Rex claimed his mom was broke, so I worked even harder to raise a monetary gift that his family was to take with them, since they could not go empty handed. This was totally wrong according to our traditions. It is the groom's family that should come up with the money for the dowry. I was paying my own dowry, but I so desperately wanted the event to be great that I didn't care.

By the time the appointed date arrived, we had saved a good amount of money. Rex sent it to his mum for the dowry to be presented to my family. I relaxed and took a deep breath. Everything was ready.

The next day I woke up early. I called my mom. I almost couldn't wait to hear the excitement in her voice as she narrated to me how the occasion went.

"Hi, Mom. How did everything go?"

"Fine." No enthusiasm in her voice at all.

I paused, waiting for her to tell me what had happened.

"Rex's mother's gift was only 2,000 Kenya Shillings."

I had given Rex's mother 80,000 Kenya Shillings to give to my mother as the introduction dowry. She gave only 2.5 percent of the amount she was to have paid, not even enough to cover the food expenses!

I have never felt so humiliated in my life. I had worked so hard to make this a great occasion, but it was a total failure. Why did Rex's family keep the money? It violated the traditions, our traditions!

Rex was at work when I received the news. I got into my car and sped off to his workplace, fuming all the way. He called his mom to find out why she didn't act as planned. "I decided it was not a good idea to give the money on the first day. We will be going back soon to visit. We will give the rest of the money then."

It wasn't her place to decide what to do with the money. Her job was to ensure our plans were carried out. She didn't involve a representative, as is custom. It was just her and her mother, Rex's grandmother. The people who were chosen to represent my family were dismayed by the turn of events. I was told they walked away shaking their heads.

To make matters worse, Rex seemed to agree with whatever his mother said. Not that he should argue, but what about what *we* wanted? What about *our* plans? Remembering the statement she made about my wanting to send "his money" to my family, I asked him if she knew that we both had worked for that money. Though he said yes, I started to doubt Rex's ability to make decisions independent of his mom.

My family had mixed feelings about the marriage. The majority of them felt that I had made a mistake to marry into that family, mainly because of the way Rex's family acted during the ceremony—as if they were doing us a favor by letting their son marry from our family. My family expected better from me. I had let them down.

I wasn't sure what kind of mess I was getting myself into, but I suspected it was bad. Worse still, I wasn't grasping that I was unwanted by Rex's family. And I wasn't ready to let go of Rex.

Being off more days than he worked, Rex spent his time catching up with his friends. Every evening he went out drinking and came home after 3 a.m. We started fighting and arguing over his drinking. He was comfortable with the little money he earned, I believe because the bills were getting paid. Before I was in his life, he worked two jobs, and all the money he saved after paying bills, he sent to his mom. Now that he wasn't making much, the share to his mom was reduced, thus confirming her fear that indeed I had stolen her son and "his money."

I decided to end the relationship and move out of Alabama. I asked a friend who drove a delivery truck around the country to drop me off in Houston, Texas. I had contacted a girlfriend from home who lived there, and she agreed to be my roommate.

I didn't tell any of this to Rex because I knew he would not let me leave. So that evening, I went home from work and waited for Rex to leave for work. Once he was gone, I could pack and leave before he returned. But to my surprise, when I got home, he was sitting outside on the patio. He pulled me gently to himself and hugged me passionately.

I was lost, because the night before we'd had a fight. He then knelt. "Please, Stella. Please don't leave me."

"What do you mean?" I was confused. I had kept my escape a secret. But, clearly, the trucker had told Rex.

"I know you plan to leave me and go to Texas. Don't leave me! I promise to change my ways and get another job."

And like a fool, I aborted my mission.

CHAPTER 6

TRIP TO KENYA

Later that year, November 2010, Rex suggested that we go home to Kenya and visit our families for Christmas. I had just come from Kenya in July 2008 and wasn't planning to return until I was done with school. We were financially not ready for such a trip, but he insisted that we needed to meet each other's families face-to-face.

We started saving money, but we could not get enough to cover two tickets and expenses, so Rex asked me to borrow money from my friend, which I did. (Later, I figured out that he had me make the loan so that only I would be responsible to repay it.) With all the inconveniences we had encountered with the traditional family introductions, I wanted to meet his family and decide for myself whether to continue with the relationship or leave.

When we arrived at Jomo Kenyatta International Airport, both families were anxiously waiting to receive us. They all stood in one area. After greetings, his family pulled him aside, and I was left with my family on the other side. I didn't pay much attention to that; besides, we were all going to the same destination. A few minutes later, we all left the airport and headed to the furnished apartment we had rented. We arrived safely, food was served, and everyone seemed happy and in a good mood.

Shortly after, I noticed that Rex and his family were all seated by the dining table. My family sat in the living room. After dinner, I thought we would all sit together as one big family and talk, get to know each other—tell them how we met and all the stories about America. But I was wrong. Rex's family wanted him to themselves and had no interest in getting to know me or my family. My family was terribly uncomfortable, and I was humiliated beyond measure. Rex acted like I didn't exist. He didn't give any attention to me or to any member of my family.

I brought gifts to his siblings, his mom, and his two grandmothers, hoping to earn their love and acceptance. They were grateful, but that didn't change the way they treated me or my family. I was especially confused by the fact that they looked down on us. I was eager to see the mansion his family lived in, for why else would they look down on us so openly? To my amazement, their economic status and ours were no different. The only difference was they lived in the city while we lived in the country. It was hard to understand why they thought themselves better.

Before we left for Kenya, we had agreed that Rex would keep all the money we had brought with us. We had also agreed on how we were going to spend it. But none of the things we had agreed on was done. We constantly argued about how and who to spend it on. Anytime it was my side of family, he had a problem, but if it was his side of family, he went all out. We hardly had any fun.

Three weeks into the vacation, I received a call from my friend in America. She sounded very excited. "A letter for you from college just arrived."

I had applied to join the nursing program before we left and had given the school my friend's address. "Open it and tell me what it says."

I heard the rattling of the paper as she ripped open the envelope. "You made it! You've been accepted into the program!"

I was overjoyed. That meant I needed to get back to the States for registration and all the necessary preparation. I shared the exciting news with Rex, but he didn't want to hear it. He didn't show any sign of excitement for my major achievement. I was very confused.

"I'll have to leave earlier than we planned, but you can stay behind if you want. I'll need to change my flight, we should have enough money to cover the cost."

"No. There's only enough left to last one more week here." He said sternly.

I was stuck. I was too embarrassed to borrow money from any family member or friend, especially since I was coming from America, what they considered "the land of milk and honey." I called the college and asked them to hold the spot for me, and I would take care of all requirements as soon as I returned. By God's grace, they agreed.

I was sure by then that I didn't want to be with this guy. For Christmas, we were supposed to go to his grandmother's in Nakuru town. After being treated like a stranger by the man who claimed to love me, I didn't care about any part of him or his family. I figured I may as well enjoy the day with my family. At least they celebrated me and enjoyed my presence. This made Rex and his family furious. By then, I didn't care about their views. I was done. I was busy strategizing in my mind how to get out of his life. But was this the right time to leave? I wondered!

CHAPTER 7

BACK TO THE USA

We had planned to move into a new apartment once we got back from our trip. All our furniture and belongings were in storage. We were to stay with my friend Ruth for a day or two while we moved. The day after we returned to the United States, I went to school and fulfilled all entrance requirements, except paying the $1,000 enrollment fee.

Later, Rex and I went to check on the apartment. They told us we had to wait one more month while they finished with the renovations. Ruth and her roommate were kind enough to let us stay with them. Meanwhile, I called every single one of my friends, hoping to borrow the $1,000 needed for school. I managed to get $300. I still needed $700.

"Rex, would you see if any of your friends could lend us some money?"

"They don't have it," he replied. I don't know if he actually asked his friends or not.

Then I remembered that we had saved $800 for rent. "Can I use the money we saved? Since we're both working and we have to wait another month to move in, that will give us enough time to save up for the apartment."

He hemmed and hawed and came up with a list of reasons why I shouldn't use that money. I could not believe it. Then in a flash it dawned on me that this guy didn't care if I started classes or not. In fact, he was making sure I didn't get in.

I remembered how he had refused to let me leave Kenya early to make sure I could register. Angry and frustrated, I gave him a choice. "If I miss this rare opportunity because you are holding on to money that we both earned, then you can go on and move into that apartment by yourself, because this is where it will all end."

He must have sensed my seriousness, for he decided to give me the money.

The classes were tough. It was like studying a foreign language. It was like nothing I had studied before. I needed full concentration to complete my studies.

On February 11, 2011, we moved into the new apartment. Although I could see the handwriting on the wall and knew this relationship was going nowhere I wanted to go, I figured that this was not the right time to end it and have to look for a roommate. I needed a stable place to stay while in school. So, I postponed leaving the relationship.

I kept my full-time job at night in a nursing home and went to school during the day. Rex, on the other hand, still worked the part-time job three days a week—Friday, Saturday, and Sunday. I urged him to look for a job since I needed to drop some hours from mine to focus on my studies. He said he would. But months passed, and he still had not found one. I wasn't even sure he was looking.

Initially, we agreed that when I was done with school, he would take a welding course. But he changed his mind, saying that he didn't like school and that he would rather start up a business. We both knew it would require us to save some money for capital. With the little we made going toward bills, we literally lived paycheck to paycheck. When we were on good terms and not arguing, we prayed together for him to get a job.

I had always wanted to be a nurse, and God made a way for that to become a reality. I wished Rex would help me achieve that goal. With the constant fights and my having to work full time while he took it easy, I believed he was determined to frustrate my efforts. Anytime we fought, he mentioned how the people who were already nurses weren't better than him anyway.

It was hard to be around someone always negating what I wanted to achieve, my heart's desire. I noticed that the longer I stayed with him, my hopes and dreams for a bigger and brighter future seemed to fade. And as they did, so did my enthusiasm for life. The only way I kept a ray of my dreams from dying completely was to constantly listen to messages of hope from Joel Osteen and Les Brown's motivational messages.

The worst part was whereas I believe we were supposed to work together as a team, I never felt included in Rex's dreams. Rather, a sense of competition existed between us and our desires. What I now know is that if someone doesn't support my dreams and aspirations, he or she is the wrong person to have in my life.

CHAPTER 8

THE HEIGHT OF ABUSE

By now, it was clear that Rex had become a drunkard, an alcoholic. He went out with his friends to drink every day he wasn't working, and he came home the following morning soaking drunk, sleeping away the entire day. My life was beyond stressful. I was working to cover most of the bills, while he partied with his friends. Anytime we were together, we argued. Some nights when I had a pending exam the next day and I was off work, I would study until 2 a.m., sleep for three hours, wake up again to study, then go to school around 8 a.m.

Rex would stumble in at 3 a.m. and demand that we make love. It didn't matter if I wanted to or not. He forced himself on me every time he came home drunk. I felt overpowered and misused. I was too embarrassed to share this problem with anyone. At school, I asked a girlfriend if it was okay for a spouse to force himself on his mate, obviously hiding the fact that it was my situation. She told me that it was illegal, whether they were married or not.

One night as this usual practice played out, I warned Rex, "If you do this again, I will report you to the authorities."

He was drunk and didn't like the sound of that.

To avoid him in his agitated state, I decided to sleep in the guest room. He stood by the door and blocked my way. "Get back to the bed."

"Please move out of the way, Rex. I don't want to fight or argue."

That made him even angrier. He slapped me so hard in the face that I staggered backward.

I could barely make sense of what he'd just done. I could not believe he'd struck me. "Did you just slap me?"

"Yes, and I will do it again if you don't get in that bed!"

He moved toward me, clearly intending to hit me again. Scared, I shouted at the top of my voice, "Help me! Someone please help me!" I wasn't sure anyone could hear me.

He threw another blow at me, but I got hold of his hand and bit his finger as hard as I could in self-defense. He screamed as he pulled his hand back. While he was distracted, I snatched my cell phone to call for help. Noticing what I was about to do, he grabbed the phone from my hand and threw it on the bed. The cell phone hit the headboard, fell onto the floor, and skidded under the bed. As he was coming back to fight me again, I heard a voice on the phone saying, "Hey, Shiru [my nickname], what's up?"

Miraculously, when the phone hit the headboard, it called the last number I had dialed. And put it on speaker! It was my friend Ruth. Relieved, I shouted, "Ruth, please hang up the phone and call the police. My life is in danger. Rex is enraged and is beating me up. Please call the police!"

"Are you serious?"

"He already hit me once. Call the police!" I heard the click indicating she'd hung up.

I was terrified of what would happen to me at that moment.

Almost a month before, I had lost a friend and workmate as a result of domestic abuse. She had confided in me how she dated a guy, and when they separated, he had a tough time letting go. He stalked her at work. Sometimes he slashed her car tires, and other times broke into her house in the middle of the night, raped her in her own bed, and threatened to kill her if she dared report it to the police. She was terrified of him.

And then one day she didn't report to work. She didn't call in either. Concerned, our supervisor called her but she did not pick up. After several failed attempts to reach her, he called a family member, who went into her house to check on her. We later received news that she had been found dead in her house, stabbed over thirty times. The guy was arrested and put in prison.

I found it hard to believe that domestic abuse could be that serious. Now I was facing and enraged man whom I called my husband. And I understood such an outcome was possible.

At that moment, it was like Rex got his senses back. He knew that Ruth would call the police. He was terrified of police. He came to where I was curled up in a corner, apologizing and saying he didn't know what had come over him. He picked me up like I was a toddler, sat on the bed, and held me on his lap. All the while I was counting the moments to when I'd hear the police at the door. I wondered why they were taking so long.

"Please don't let them take me to jail. I will never put my hand on you again," he pleaded.

Twenty minutes later, the knock finally came. He squeezed me to himself and begged for forgiveness one more time. When I opened the door, I was both happy and disappointed. Ruth had decided to come instead of calling the cops. Apparently, she didn't think I was serious.

We all sat down and started talking. Rex said he was drunk and that he was sorry he reacted like that. I agreed not to involve the cops, but I refused to stay in the same house with him. I left with my friend. On our way to her house, I explained how he had been treating me lately. I told her that I wasn't planning on going back to him. She agreed with me and said I was free to stay with her if I wanted.

We went straight to the emergency room because my jaw was hurting so bad from the slap, I thought it was broken. After admission, the doctor asked how I had attained the injury. I lied that a door had hit me. I could tell that he knew I was lying by the way he looked at me. It was obvious I had been crying. He excused himself and left the room. Ruth remained outside in the waiting area.

When the doctor came back, a police officer accompanied him. The doctor told me that he suspected I was not telling him the truth. I broke down in tears. The police officer stepped closer and asked if I had been abused. I didn't answer him. I didn't have to. He must have encountered such issues before. He started writing a statement, asking for details: the name of the abuser, the address, and his physical appearance. It may sound odd, but as I answered, a wave of guilt swept over me because I had promised Rex not to tell. The officer left, and the doctor treated my injury. Thankfully, my jaw was still intact. But emotionally I was far from being okay. I would keep that scar forever.

I missed class the following day, which was nursing clinicals day, because my emotions were in a jumble. Later that day, a friend I went to school with called. "Why didn't you attend clinicals? Our teacher was concerned and asked about you."

I gave a noncommittal answer that seemed to satisfy her.

Lucky for me, it was a Friday. I counted on the weekend to get myself together.

Monday morning, my Pharmacology lecturer called me aside in the hallway. "I noticed that your grades are slipping and you missed a very important class."

All she was saying was true, and I tried my best to compose myself. "Yes ma'am. I am okay. I will try harder to improve my grades."

She looked at me skeptically, clearly not buying my answer. "Are you sure everything is okay?"

Tears trickled down my cheeks, betraying the smile I attempted to apply on my face. At that point, she held me by my shoulders and directed me to an empty classroom, where I told her everything.

She was concerned about my safety and well-being and took matters into her hands by involving campus police. She asked me to bring Rex's picture to them in case he came looking for me at school. She also suggested going to a women's shelter, but I told her that I was okay living with a friend. I took out a restraining order against him as she recommended. He was not allowed to call, text, or come anywhere near me. If I saw him, I was to call the police and report him.

The police went to his address but didn't find him there. He had escaped. But then a week into my stay at Ruth's house, he started calling several times a day. I ignored his calls and later blocked his number. But I never reported his violation of the restraining order.

There was and still is stigma in our Kenyan community regarding reporting someone for abuse. The victim, not the abuser, is considered the bad guy. That was why I didn't want to report him in the first place. When he came by with a bouquet of flowers, I spotted him from inside the house through the window. I ignored him till he left. Sometimes Ruth went outside and asked him to leave. He would plead for forgiveness. Then he started calling every one of my friends and family members, telling them how wrong he was, how miserable my absence had made him, and how his life was nothing without me.

I had made up my mind. I was done with him. But some of my friends and family members gave in to his pleas. Some even told me they had endured more than a slap in their own marriages. None of them, including my family, knew about the rapes, and I was too embarrassed to tell anyone about that part of the abuse. Pressure came from everywhere, convincing me that I was going to lose a good man.

One day as I left work and walked to my car in the parking lot with some ladies I worked with, I looked up and saw Rex standing by my car, holding a large bouquet of roses. As we got closer, he knelt like he was about to propose. My friends held their hands over their mouths with excitement. "OMG, Stella!" I didn't want to expose my problems to them, so I acted like I was thrilled, too. When they left, I threw the roses away and asked him to leave.

He begged so hard that I was convinced he was a changed man. I foolishly chose to give him another chance.

CHAPTER 9

"HONEYMOON" AGAIN

Life looked and felt good after I went back to Rex. He had found a new and better job with more hours and benefits. He was excited about it, and I was happy for him. I hoped that stress was an issue of the past. I also managed to get an easier job in which I sat with elderly patients in their homes or nursing home rooms. I liked the job because while the patients slept, I could study for my classes and exams.

In December 2011, my dream came true: I graduated from nursing school. Rex seemed happy for me. He made a comment that caught me by surprise. "You are either too smart, or God loves you so much, if you actually passed." I asked why he said that. "Because there was too much stress that I didn't expect you to make it."

"I think it's both. I know God loves me so much that He made me smart," I said. I realized that all the fights Rex caused were intended to ensure that I failed.

We went for the pinning ceremony, an event held by the campus for the graduating nurses. I remember the look of disappointment in the eyes of my Pharmacology teacher when she saw me with Rex. She had told me that I deserved better than an abusive man. And I knew she was right. But at that moment, I held out hope and I prayed that Rex would prove to be a changed man.

In the beginning of 2012, while studying and preparing for the board of nursing exam, I was practicing nursing with a temporary license. Both Rex and I worked the night shift and met at home in the morning. One day, I called Rex on my way home, as it was my usual practice. He meant to hit the End button when we'd finished talking, but he mistakenly pressed the Answer button, keeping the connection open. I listened in fascinated horror as I overheard a woman talking to him. "What are you going to do with Stella if you want to marry me?" Why would your mother prefer me over Stella, considering I smoke and drink, while Stella is a church girl?"

"Oh, my goodness!" I exclaimed after I disconnected the call. I couldn't believe what I was hearing. I was scheduled for a replacement, and I had no idea. I couldn't wait for the explanation from Rex, starting with how his mom never approved of me in the first place. How was he planning to get rid of me? He was having an affair barely six months after I'd given him another chance to be in my life. To say that I felt stupid is an understatement.

When he arrived home, I confronted him, and he totally denied he was involved with anyone. But he continued seeing the other girl behind my back. I knew because he would leave his job at the end of his shift but not come home.

What was I supposed to do while I waited for them to work their relationship/marriage? Is this the point where I fight or take flight? I was confused.

Eventually, something must have happened, because he quit seeing her. I ignored his "indiscretion," forgave him, and prayed for strength.

Rex's partying habits never changed, though. He was either at work or out with friends. I grew used to being alone at home. On weekends, I would get a bottle of wine and drink myself to sleep on the couch. He would come home drunk to find a drunk wife passed out in the living room. The wine seemed to drown my stress and numb the pain of abandonment. But it was only temporary relief, because when I sobered up, my situation remained unchanged. I was stuck in a dysfunctional marriage, and I didn't have enough courage to get out of it.

Shortly after his affair, I discovered I was pregnant. We were both overjoyed by the news. I was certain that Rex would get serious and commit to role of husband and father. I stopped drinking and focused on keeping our unborn child healthy.

In June 2012, I sat for my board exam, and thankfully, I passed. I was finally a licensed nurse. My dream fully realized! I looked for a more permanent and better paying job. I was fortunate to find a position at a nursing home facility as a skilled nurse.

Here, I met a friendly older lady, Shila. She was very nice to me, and even though she was much older than I was, we quickly struck up a friendship. We were together at work and even out of work. We visited each other's houses. I met her two daughters and a granddaughter. All of them were very kind and welcoming. She helped me to shop for our unborn baby. Eventually I introduced her to Rex.

My hope that my pregnancy would tame Rex was just a wish, as wistful as a puff of smoke on a windy day. Rather than subdue his partying ways, his carousing increased. Before I got pregnant when we'd fight, he would try to settle it and make peace, but once I got pregnant, he didn't care if I was upset. He would walk away and go about his business. To him, my being with child meant I was chained to his life forever. Even if I left him, our child connected us.

As I got to know Shila more, I trusted her enough to share what was happening in my home. She was very supportive and encouraged me to be strong for the sake of my unborn child. She recommended that I focus on the child and not the dad.

Imagining that I was about to give birth in a dysfunctional environment really stressed me. I tried to talk to Rex about it and even invited a mutual friend, who was a counselor, to talk to him. It never worked. He had lost all care in the world. I hated that my decision to stay in his life despite all the ill treatments he had given me had resulted to a very unhealthy home environment. If I had left earlier, I would probably have been happier and far less stressed. During my prenatal visits, my doctor strongly advised me to relieve what was causing my stress because my blood pressure was going through the roof. She said I could give birth prematurely if I didn't do something about my stress level. Telling Rex about it was like talking to a stone. It didn't bother him one bit.

A friend from home called while I was crying over the issue. I narrated what I was going through. He talked some sense into my head by reminding me how hardworking I was and how the worst thing I could do was let this guy affect the health of the baby by bringing his chaos into my life. He spoke a truth that totally changed my outlook. "Maybe it's time you start seeing yourself as a single mother and focus on the baby's well-being." That was the best advice anyone could have given. His words were a turning point for me! My attitude changed. I decided to do my best by ignoring what was going on around me.

In March 2013, I gave birth to our daughter. She was as healthy as could be, thanks be to God. It was more than a blessing to hold my bundle of joy. I stayed home for three months, being with her and healing from a C-section. We tried to bring my mother in-law to the United States to help with the baby, but we were not able to. I returned to work and changed my shift to mornings instead of nights.

Raising a child is usually a shared responsibility between parents, especially here in the States, where parents work in shifts. We had a very nice lady who watched the baby in her home. Sometimes Rex could watch her in the morning because he worked nights. At 3 p.m., I would rush home to relieve him so he could rest before his night shift. We did that for a while, and all seemed well.

Then the situation changed. Rex started working late, and I'd have to drop the baby off early before heading to work. At first, I didn't mind. We had another mouth to feed, and we obviously needed more money, which meant one of us had to work more hours. But later it seemed like it was only my responsibility to drop off and pick up our daughter while still working full time. Rex excluded himself from all baby duties. He came and went as he pleased. I didn't know what days he did or didn't work. When I insisted that he stay with the baby, he became upset. From that time, anytime I came home, our daughter would be playing in her baby walker while Rex was sprawled on the couch watching TV.

I never once found her in his arms. He never played with her or read her books. As soon as I stepped into the house, Rex would either go to bed or leave the house.

My daughter would scream for my attention. She wouldn't let me put her down once I picked her up. Sometimes I had to carry her on my back as I prepared dinner or did other household chores. Clearly, she needed to feel a physical connection to her parents, but she didn't seem to be getting it from Rex.

Rex became a stranger to us, his family, and spent most of his free time drinking with his friends. We argued about our daughter all the time, and sometimes he would shout, push me, and bang doors in anger. She was becoming terrified of him. Other times we barely talked to each other. Shila was there at times and observed it all.

One day, obviously unable to hold it in anymore, Shila told me I deserved someone who would treat me better than Rex did. I confided in her that I always hoped my children would have a father in their lives, which was why I didn't want to leave the marriage. But I knew that Rex was not acting like the father my daughter deserved. In fact, she was to all intents and purposes fatherless. Was it better to be completely without a father, or to have one who shows no care in the world for you?

I acknowledged that to raise my child in a loveless, toxic marriage wasn't doing her any favor. I grew up without a father, but the difference was that I knew he loved me when he was there.

The relationship between Rex and me became unbearable. He called me names and put me down at every opportunity. He told me how he'd met several other beautiful women and that he could replace me anytime he wanted. Tired of hearing his insults, I formulated a strategy as to how to leave him. I would suffer dire consequences if he knew I even thought of leaving. So, I never mentioned it.

Even though I wanted my daughter to have a father in her life, whether we were separated or not, I was sure that Rex was not like other fathers who easily and willingly paid child support, which is the law here in America. He hated the expression "child support" and believed that the mothers who received it didn't use the money on the child but spent it on themselves to enjoy the company of other men. To be honest, I wasn't worried about his financial support but for our safety. I could work three jobs if I had to.

Sometime back, I was at a friend's baby shower, and there was a story going around about a Kenyan man who was separated from his baby's mama, also Kenyan. He paid child support but his visits with his daughter had to be supervised. One night, though, around 1 a.m., he went to his ex-wife's house and requested that she let him see the baby. He said he was traveling and wouldn't be able to see the child for a while. She let him in. When he got into the house, she saw that he was armed with a knife. He chased her around the house. Miraculously, she managed to run out of the house with "only" a few stab wounds. She rushed to the neighbors and asked them to call the police. Meanwhile, her daughter was still inside the house, sleeping on the couch. By the time the police arrived, they found the girl's dad kneeling over her, stabbing her repeatedly. They shot and killed him on-site. The daughter was pronounced dead at the hospital.

Disturbed by the details of the story, I shared it with Rex when I got home. But his reaction shocked me even more than the tragic story. He shook his head. "That guy is so stupid. Why would he kill his own baby? Why not just kill the mother?"

Dumbfounded, I asked, "You mean it's okay to kill the mother?"

He tried to explain himself and rephrase his words to sound nonthreatening. But I knew he could do just what he said. The words from Bible popped into my memory: "O generation of vipers, how can ye, being evil, speak good things? For out of the abundance of the heart the mouth speaketh" (Matt. 12: 34 KJV).

How could I safely raise my child and have the father involved without being in constant fear for my life? I had overstayed my "welcome," and in so doing, I had put both my life and my daughter's in danger.

The ironic thing was, to the outside world, we seemed like a happy couple. I was sure to wear a smile anytime I was outside my home. No one suspected the dysfunction in my family. It's amazing the lies and horrors a smile can cover.

Abuse is an embarrassing topic to share with others. And the one friend I had attempted to tell about it, apart from Shila, didn't seem to understand my predicament, even though she had been abused herself. She advised that he would stop at some point, like she claimed her husband did. But our situation was not improving and was, in fact, moving from bad to worse. There were all sorts of news within our Kenyan community, of men killing their wives and kids then going to prison or killing themselves. This seemed especially true of Kenyans living abroad. I prayed I would not someday be on the news.

As I plotted ways to become independent and free from this prison called marriage, I shared every detail with Shila. She helped me see the blind spots. I was so grateful she was in my life. Having escaped abuse in her previous marriage afforded her more experience and wisdom than I had. With time, I gained enough courage and faith that I could survive and even thrive as a single mom.

Then all hell broke loose.

CHAPTER 10

THE LAST STRAW

When our daughter was five months old, Rex came home one day from work and told me that we needed to travel to Kenya in a month so his mother could see the baby. "Are you serious?" I figured he must be joking. "The baby is too young to travel, and I haven't fully recovered from the C-section. Plus, I just resumed work, and I am sure they won't allow more time off."

He insisted that we go.

"How do you plan to get the money? Why the rush? Is Mom okay?" I asked.

"She is okay, but she wants to see the baby soon. Don't worry about the money. My mom will take care of everything."

Recalling how I had to beg for money from him the last time we traveled, I could not trust him, much less his mom, with me and our infant daughter. I was not going to drop everything and go home penniless, so I tried to reason with him. "Why don't you go see your mom and then later, when the baby is at least a year old, we can go together?"

He wasn't having it.

I called his mom and tried to explain the situation. I realized she was pressuring him and wouldn't listen to me.

That's when everything got worse. Rex went mute on me and the baby. I tried to resolve the issue on several occasions, but he just shrugged his shoulders and went about his business.

I didn't understand why it was so important to go home unprepared. What was the emergency, and why was it such a big issue? Two weeks went by without our talking. I was used to being a single mom while still "married." He walked in and out of the house at his convenience. Home life got strange and even a bit scary. It was clear he didn't care about either of us. Sometimes my daughter would cry while she fixed her eyes on her daddy, obviously seeking his attention. But he would ignore her and walk off. I felt he was using our child to punish me.

Around this time, my mother called me one morning and told me to take all my important documents and get them out of the house to a safe place. She didn't explain much, just that she had a bad feeling. She made sure I did exactly as she had ordered. Her warning added to my anxiety and fear.

I knew for sure that I was on my way out, hopefully, not through death. If by divorce or separation, I knew the law in America concerning parenting and how both parents share custody of and responsibility in raising children, whether together or separated. The only problem with shared custody was I knew that Rex's threats would impact my daughter's safety as well as mine.

As I pondered what I had to do and worried about our well-being, I knew I couldn't handle the enormity of my situation. I needed divine intervention. I had often knelt next to my bed, and with tears of rejection and abandonment rolling down my face, I prayed for God to change the situation. But my prayers had not been answered. My circumstances were changing only in one direction—worse! I wondered why God had not answered my pleas.

Nevertheless, I decided to try one more time. When I knelt that day, I literally cried my heart out to God. I knew If He didn't hear and answer me this time, then something tragic could happen. A feeling of doom hovered over me. My back was hard pressed against the wall and I knew that only God would rescue me.

I prayed.

"Heavenly Dad, I'm here this evening, first wanting to repent for all the wrongs I've done. And I receive Your forgiveness. You have turned a deaf ear to all the prayers I've prayed over my marriage. Nothing has changed. In fact, things are getting worse. But I also confess that I

didn't consult Your counsel before getting into this marriage. You tried to get my attention, but I didn't listen.

"I confess that I have wronged You. But You are full of mercy. In Your great mercies, please hear me. The Bible tells me that if we repent our sins and call on Your name, you will hear us and answer our prayers. So, heavenly Dad, in the name of Your Son, Jesus Christ, I pray that You hear me today.

"I tried to make things work on my own. I thought I could change Rex. I understand that it was not my call to change him in the first place. But, Dad, I have no strength left. All my efforts have failed. I am at the end of myself. And I want to leave it to You. But if things don't change from now on, I don't think I can survive it. I pray, Dad, that You guide me from here. If Rex is my husband, I ask that You change him or the situation. But if this marriage was never Your will for me, I ask that You make a way out of it. Please, Dad, I have read in the Bible how You made a way through the Red Sea for the Israelites and saved them from their oppressors. You have made ways in my own life before, and You still can. So, Dad, please show me a sign of whether You want me to stay or leave. I promise I will listen to You this time.

"And one more thing, Dad. Please give me a clear sign that I can understand. If You put a rainbow in the sky or send a dove onto the balcony, I won't know what You mean by that. So, please make a drastic change in Rex like You did with Saul in the Bible if you mean for me to stay, *or a clear way out if you want me to leave so I won't have any doubts. It is in the name of Jesus that I pray this and believe. Amen."*

I knew God heard my prayer, because I felt a peace in my heart. I stopped stressing and waited for the sign I had asked for. I was observant of any changes so I wouldn't miss the sign.

It was November 2013, the weekend before Thanksgiving holiday. I was expecting some friends with whom we had formed a women's empowerment group. We would contribute a certain amount of money—$200 per person, per month—and one of us would receive it. The cycle continued until all members were covered, and then we started again. It was my turn to receive the money and host the group.

Around this same time Rex started talking to me. He was very nice to our daughter and stayed around the house. I had woken up to the fact that anytime I had some money, especially tax returns, he would hang around and be extra nice to me—only because he wanted the money. After the money was gone, he would return to his usual self. *Not this time!*

That Friday morning before my women's group meeting, he came home around 9 a.m. I was startled when he said, "We need to talk." He had never said that, and I never expected it in my lifetime. He didn't look upset, so I knew it wasn't anything bad. We talked, well . . . he did most of the talking.

"I haven't been the best partner to you or father to our daughter. I want to change, but I don't know how. Maybe we should visit a marriage counselor."

My heart almost leaped out of my body. *Did he just say marriage counselor?* I had suggested the idea numerous times, but he always opposed it. *Could this be the sign I prayed for?*

"When do you plan for us to see a counselor?" I asked.

"After Thanksgiving weekend."

I agreed but didn't show much emotion. I was used to him saying one thing and doing the opposite. Lying was natural to him.

The meeting with the ladies went well on Saturday. When they left, I was $2,000 richer. I hid the money in one of my baby's shoes. On Sunday evening, Rex asked if he could borrow $400 for a personal need. I thought to myself, here we go! I lied that I had sent the money to a family member on my way from church, so I couldn't help him. He obviously didn't like that, but he was careful not to show it.

That night he went to work. As we talked on the phone during his lunch break, he said something I thought was unusual. He told me about a workmate who was caught at work with drugs. I knew the guy. Rex said the guy would serve time in jail and had already been fired from his job.

In dismay, I asked, "Why would he risk losing such a good job and go to jail just for some drugs?"

"Going to jail is not too bad as long as you accomplish your mission," he said.

I was lost for a second. A mission? "What mission? What do you mean?"

"Gotta go. My lunch break is over." Then he hung up the phone.

As I cleaned up that evening, my mind wandered around that word *mission*. It didn't make sense regarding the matter we were discussing. I decided that I would ask him when he came home in the morning, and I went to bed.

Monday morning arrived, he came home from work and entered the master bedroom where our daughter and I were sleeping. It was around 6 a.m. and still dark. He changed his work clothes and left. A while later, I heard him come back into the room. I didn't open my eyes, but by instinct, I felt a presence near me. Opening my eyes, I saw him standing by the bed staring at us. My daughter was breastfeeding and was lying next to me. Startled, I whispered, "Is everything okay?"

"Yes."

I went back to sleep.

He then picked up my cell phone from the bedside table and took a few pictures of us sleeping. The camera flash woke me up. "What are you doing?"

"You guys look beautiful. I just wanted a picture." He then left the room.

Still half asleep, I didn't think how weird that was, considering that he hated pictures and he rarely took pictures of us unless I insisted.

When I got up later that morning, I totally forgot to continue our conversation from the previous night. The rest of the day seemed to pass uneventfully.

Little did I know of the storm that way coming my way.

CHAPTER 11

THE HORRIFIC EVENT

Tuesday, November 26, 2013, will remain etched in my memory. It was the most horrific day and yet one of the best days of my life.

Before going to work, I had to visit a friend who was in a rehabilitation center due to stroke. I was to leave home around 10:30 a.m., earlier than usual. I had told Rex about it the night before.

In the morning, he came home, and, as usual, as I dozed before getting up. I heard him coming in and out of the room. Normally, he limited movement in our bedroom because our daughter's crib was by our bed. She was a light sleeper. But that day, Rex kept coming in and out of the room, asking what time I was going to wake up. I whispered, "Nine a.m." I had not fallen asleep till 3 a.m. "Don't worry. I have already set the alarm."

He said okay and left the room.

I glanced at the clock: 7:30 a.m. I closed my eyes, hoping I could catch some more sleep. What seemed like only ten minutes later, he came back into the bedroom. In fact, he continued for the next hour slipping in and out of the room. Then he came in and laid next to me, supporting his head with his arm and staring at me. I was getting upset because he kept waking me up. By then, the natural light lit the room. "What's going on?" I asked.

He shook his head. "Well, it's almost nine a.m."

I looked at my clock. It was 8:45. For a split second, I thought he wanted to make love to me; why else was he so anxious? But he didn't do or say anything to indicate this intention.

I sat up and told him I was going to shower. He stopped me. "I found water on the kitchen floor. Did you use the dishwasher the previous night?"

It had been leaking when turned on, so I couldn't use it. I assured him that I had not. I went to the kitchen and saw that there was water on the floor, but it was clean water. I wondered how that had happened. When the dishwasher leaked, it was soapy, foamy water.

A bubbling caught my attention. A pot of water was boiling on the stove. I assumed Rex wanted to make hot tea, which we normally had for breakfast. I mopped the floor dry and then went to the bathroom to take my shower.

By then, our daughter had woken up. I asked Rex to watch her while I got ready. He picked her from her crib and put her in her highchair in the living room in front of the TV. He then put on her favorite cartoon show and raised the TV volume to maximum. It obviously startled her, so she screamed in fear. Hearing how loud it was and how it scared her, I tried to call to him from the bathroom to turn it down. He lowered the volume a little, but it was still loud enough for me to hear over the shower water. He gave the baby some formula, which distracted and calmed her.

I was almost done with my shower when he walked into the bathroom. He used the toilet then flushed it, but I didn't hear him leave the room. I felt his presence. He wasn't moving or saying anything. Opening the shower curtain slightly, I peeked and saw him standing still, staring at himself in the mirror, obviously lost in thought. "Are you okay?"

He said yes and left the bathroom. Looking back now, I see how his actions were unusual and out of place. But at the time I didn't make much of it at all.

When I finished, I dressed up in my scrub pants and a tank top. I intended to breastfeed our daughter before getting fully dressed. I went to the kitchen for breakfast. Rex was sitting by the kitchen island, and the baby was nearby on the floor. He had a little bucket with water in it, and a washcloth in his hand pressed to his left knee. He told me he'd hurt himself at work. I took a brief look at the knee and saw no swelling or bruising. It didn't look serious, and so I went on to prepare breakfast.

Looking over, I saw the pot of water still boiling on the stove. I asked what the water was for. He said it was for his knee. I turned off the burner and moved the pot from the front burner to the back one, just in case my crawling daughter went close to the stove.

"I made a cup of tea for you and put it in the microwave," Rex said.

I thanked him then stepped to the microwave. I picked up my cup of tea, a piece of toast, and was headed to the dining room when he called from behind me.

"Babe, look!"

I turned around to look at him. He was standing by the stove. In his right hand was the pot of boiling water I had just moved. Within a split second, he picked up the pot and swung it toward my face!

"Oh, my God!" I shouted.

By reflex reaction I lifted my left hand, which was holding the toast, to my face. I screamed in shock as the hot water hit my bare skin. The pain was incredible. I stared at Rex in disbelief, trying to make sense of what had just happened. He stood at the same spot, still holding on to the empty pot in his hand and staring at me, probably assessing the extent of the burns.

Hearing me scream, the baby, who was crawling toward me just inches away, started screaming also. The whole place erupted in chaos. Rex seemed confused. He threw the empty pot near my feet and tried to fake a fall, which wasn't very successful.

"OH MY GOD!!! What did you just do?" I yelled.

"Sorry, babe, it was an accident."

"What?" I said, shocked. "I watched you throw the boiling water on me."

"No. It was an accident."

Feeling like my whole face and chest was on fire, I stood in a daze. My mind was brainstorming all kinds of questions. Was this really happening? Was it happening to me? What was next? Is this how people get killed? Was this my day to die? If so, what would happen to my baby, or would he kill her, too?

While these questions raced through my mind, I couldn't move. I waited to see what Rex would do next. He was standing next to the drawer we kept the knives in. I hoped to God that he wouldn't remember that.

As I began to regain my senses, I realized that he had planned doing this all along, hence the rush to get me out of bed, the water on kitchen floor where he was trying to fake a fall, the picture taken in bed the day before—I believe to compare the before and after when his plan was completed. My first instinct told me that this guy was capable of being much more cunning than this, especially if he thought the law was would become involved in investigating my "accident."

I believe the Lord intervened and gave me wisdom when I said, trying to keep my voice as calm as possible,

"Please call the ambulance, because accident or not, I'm burning up here and I need to go to the hospital." Looking down at my chest, my skin was peeling off, leaving my flesh bare and raw. He picked up his cell phone from the kitchen island and started punching numbers. I was close enough to read the screen. He'd dialed 1-1-9!

I didn't say a word. I slowly walked into the bedroom, took my cell phone from the bedside table and dialed 9-1-1. I was careful what I said. "I need help. I just got burnt." The operator asked several questions, but I said it was an accident.

I felt Rex breathing from behind me, obviously listening in. He grabbed the phone from my hand before I could give them the address. "I'll give them the address. Just go and get ready before they get here."

Fearfully, I obeyed.

After he finished, he picked up the baby from the high chair in the living room where he had put her. She had been crying the whole time. A minute after he left the room, my phone rang. It was Emergency Medical Services (EMS) asking for the address. I gave it to them and the caller asked, "So who was the person who gave us the wrong address and why?" I apologized, fully aware what was going on. I asked them to hurry.

I also called Shila and told her that I had just gotten burned. I was careful not to indicate that Rex meant to do it, in case he overheard me. I heard her yell her daughter's name and say, "Oh my God, Rex just burnt Stella!" I was surprised at how she knew the details of what had transpired. I didn't mention Rex. How could she have been so insightful? But I didn't have the luxury of time to think about that.

Within less than five minutes, which seemed like an eternity, EMS knocked at the door. It was the most important knock of my life. It assured me that I was going to live, scarred or not! Rex held the baby as the EMS escorted me to the ambulance. He wanted to ride with us in the ambulance, probably to make sure that I stuck with the story of the accident. But they told him he couldn't because he had the baby. He told me he was going to drive right behind the ambulance to the hospital.

As soon as the ambulance drove off, the guy tending to me looked me straight in my eyes. "This was not an accident, was it?" Knowing that he might call the police immediately, I confided in him that it was not but pleaded with him not to inform the authorities until I was sure the baby was safely out of Rex's hands. With his promise that he would, we rushed to the hospital.

Along the way I had all these thoughts going through my head. "Lord! I don't want to have scars on my face. Will I have a scary look and will people be staring at me everywhere I go?"

CHAPTER 12

SCARRED FOR LIFE OR WHAT?

The Emergency Room they took me into was crowded with ten doctors wearing white coats, a couple of nurses in scrubs, and two policemen. Seeing all those doctors made it clear that the situation was more serious than I first thought. As soon as I was transferred to the only bed in the room, the doctors surrounded me. One assessed my face. A nurse poked me in my left arm as she started an IV, while three doctors examined my chest. Before I could breathe in and out, I was on morphine for the excruciating pain. Someone cleaned and bandaged my chest. Two doctors assessed my eyes then poured cold liquid into them.

"How bad is my face?"

The doctor who was assessing my face answered. "You have suffered first-degree burns in the face and left arm, and second-degree burns on your chest. Don't worry about your face. I'm confident you will fully recover."

Before I could ask anything else, the doctor tending my eyes interrupted. "You're extremely lucky that the boiling water didn't get into your eyes. Had that occurred, it would have caused instant blindness."

"Are you serious?"

"Absolutely."

At that moment, I realized just how much God loved me to have protected my sight. I was so grateful to God that I didn't care about any scarring that might occur on my face.

The doctors finished their initial assessment, hooked me up to a monitor, then left the room. The two police officers stepped closer, one with a paper and pen ready to jot down my statement. Before they could ask me any questions, I requested that they please get my daughter to a safe place. I believe I was shaking as I spoke, because one officer patted me lightly on my right arm and told me not to worry, that my baby would be fine. The other officer left the room.

Somehow, he sounded convincing enough and I stayed calm. As I narrated everything that happened in detail, he wrote it down. When he finished questioning me, a lady dressed in a gray pantsuit walked into the room. She introduced herself and said she was from Child Protective Services (CPS). Immediately, my heart skipped a few beats. I was afraid of what else she would say. "Do you have any family members who could keep your daughter while you're in the hospital?"

"No, but my friend has been babysitting for me. She'll take her." I gave her my friend's information.

"I'll visit your friend and determine if her home is suitable for your daughter."

"What if it's not? What will happen to her?"

"In that case, we will place your baby in foster care until you are well enough to get her back."

That was the last thing I needed to hear. I prayed a silent prayer for God not to allow that to happen.

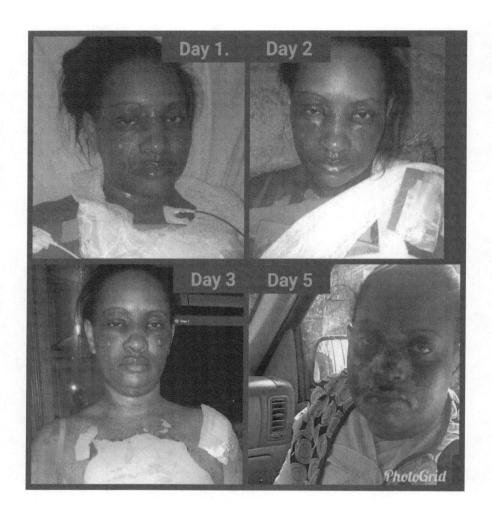

Meanwhile, Shila arrived at the hospital. She took my daughter from Rex, who was in the waiting room, and came in to see me. Rex was not allowed to come in.

My baby was crying for me. She wanted to breastfeed, but I was not able to even hold her. My chest and breasts were bandaged up. I was engorged with milk, but I couldn't nurse her or even pump the milk.

I was upset that I could not feed or hold my own child. I felt bitter, helpless, and sad. How could Rex be so selfish, not to think of his own daughter? Breastfeeding was my time to bond with my baby. It was my favorite part of parenting. And now, he had snatched it away from both of us.

It was after I was left alone in the ER room that I fired off a series of questions to God. *"God, why did You let this happen? How come You didn't protect me? You promised that You will never leave me nor forsake me, but if feels like You did."*

My string of questions and complaints allowed no break for Him to answer me. When I got tired of talking, I felt a well of hot tears forming in my eyes. My heart was broken. I was confused about which way to go and who to trust with my life. Right at that moment, when I felt like my whole world was collapsing under my feet, the Holy Spirit brought to my remembrance the prayer I had prayed, asking for direction and a clear sign. I was perplexed by the thought. Then goose bumps raised on my skin. I looked up and asked God amid my tears, "You mean this was the sign? Like, seriously, all this was a sign?" And I felt like God was smiling back at me saying, "You asked for it, didn't you?"

That very moment, I felt a warmth in my body and unexplainable peace like nothing I had experienced before. My attitude immediately changed from fear and hopelessness to peace, joy, and freedom. I figured that if

God allowed it to happen, then He must have a way out for me. I was completely relaxed from that point on.

That day, Rex was taken into custody, awaiting investigation. I was discharged from the hospital the same evening, along with prescription drugs and care instructions for my wounds.

Even though I was worried about my final look, a sense of freedom and joy filled my heart. I knew I had, broken out of "prison". I was ready for the next chapter of my life, but meanwhile where do I go?

CHAPTER 13

HOMELESSNESS

After my discharge from the hospital, I woke up to the reality that I didn't have a home to go to. Going back to our apartment was not an option because I didn't know how long Rex would be in custody and how he might threaten me or my baby.

It is funny how in one instant your life can change. I was married the night before, but now I was not only single, I was a single mother of an infant daughter and homeless! Shila took in both me and my child. May God forever bless her!

My friends who had heard about my attack called and came by to check on me. They expected me to be discouraged and downcast, but they heard and saw the opposite. I made jokes about my ugly face, and we all laughed. I'm sure they thought I was suffering from post-traumatic stress, but I was just happy to know that God had my back and that my misery was over.

One of my friends convinced me to post a photo of my burned self on Facebook to alert people about the risks of being in an abusive relationship. At first, I was against the idea because it was sure to attract attention to me: sympathy and all kinds of emotional responses. But she convinced me that we needed to warn people of how dangerous abusive marriages are. So, I posted my picture.

Within moments, people I didn't know wrote consoling messages on my Facebook page. It was such a good feeling to read people's words of encouragement and empathy. Some offered prayers, but most of all, many people wanted to know what I had done to trigger Rex to such a reaction. There were all kinds of speculations, some that made me sick to my stomach. My enemies were jumping up and down. They were sure that was the end of me!

But God still had my back!

My mom and siblings were devastated by the news, especially because they were so far away and couldn't be there for and with me. I talked to my mom regularly, assuring her that I was doing fine, but after seeing the photo on Facebook, she was not convinced. At one point, I applied layers of makeup and took a picture to send her to assure her that I was okay. I was afraid she would get sick with worry.

Staring at my disfigured face in the mirror, it dawned on me that I had never really appreciated my looks before. I repented and asked God for a second chance. I promised never to take anything for granted.

While Rex remained in custody a few days after I left the hospital, a police officer accompanied me to my home to gather my things. As I packed, I thought about how many tears I had cried in that apartment. How many lonely nights I had spent there, how many fights we'd had. But most important, I recalled the last prayer I'd said in that house. The one that was answered by fire!

I packed my clothes, my daughter's clothes, and left everything else. I needed a fresh start. If we had to sleep on the floor for a while, it was well worth our peace of mind.

A week later, Rex was released from custody. I had filed a restraining order against him, which he knew about. But that didn't stop him from calling. I blocked his phone number. He started calling Shila, begging her to talk me into forgiving him. I made it clear to her that I didn't want anything to do with him. I asked her to stop entertaining his calls. When she didn't listen to me, I decided to ignore it.

One time, he came to her house and brought some gifts. I refused them and asked him to take them back. My daughter, oblivious of what was going on was just crawling on the floor, not paying attention to him. After he left, Shila came into the bedroom where I was sitting on the bed. "It's okay to let him buy you gifts." She said.

"No, it is not! I'm not interested in accepting anything from him. You can keep them. Please do not let him come back. I'm afraid of what he could do to me or our daughter."

I knew he was using the gifts as bait. He never once bought me or our daughter a gift before while we were a family. Buying them now was not only someone else's idea, but it was the wrong time. The cord was cut, and nothing he could say or do would lure me back into his cruel hands.

To my bewilderment, Shila seemed to be in a neutral position, not sure whether to be fully on my side or his. I wondered why she didn't see the danger she was putting everyone in. Living in her house meant that I was also at her mercy. I could not insist on anything, much less who she chose to bring into her home. I was afraid she might throw me and my daughter out.

Once again, I felt unsafe.

CHAPTER 14

NEW BEGINNINGS

My intention was to go back to work, make as much money as I could, and leave Alabama. I had seen and been through so much in that state that one more day in it felt like I was sitting on fire.

Three days after I left the hospital, the wounds on my chest became infected, and I had to go back to the hospital. I spent two nights there and was then released. A week after I left hospital, I went back for checkup and asked the doctor to write a note allowing me back to work. He did, and I resumed working. I had to wear T-shirts under my uniform to cover the bandages that were still on my chest.

My workmates, who by now had heard all about the tragedy, looked at me with pity in their eyes. I could not stand it. Sympathy has never done me any good. I don't even know how to pity myself. I guess that came from being a tomboy while growing up. I'd fall, get up, dust off, and keep going. I needed enough money to get me out of that doomed state, not sympathy.

Two weeks into the job, I tried to act like I was okay. But the stress I was under proved to be too much. I was fired for making a mistake. It felt like the world was conspiring against me. Luckily, I had a part-time job and worked one to two shifts a pay period as needed. By God's grace, when I called the supervisor to see if I was needed, she replied that they were overloaded with work and needed all the help I could offer. This ended up being a blessing because this part-time job paid me more money than my full-time nursing job I had lost. With the overtime, I easily and quickly managed to save up money.

Some of my church members and friends also raised money to help me restart my life. I will forever be grateful for their help. By February 2014, I had most of my furniture I had purchased on layaway fully paid and into storage. I had also managed to secure an apartment online in Houston, Texas. I was ready to go.

Thankfully, Shila volunteered to help me move. I rented a U-Haul truck, loaded my belongings, and hooked my car to the back. Shila, myself, and my infant daughter embarked on a journey that I hoped would be a new dawn in my life. I believed that my years of Egypt—a form of slavery that my relationship had become—were over and I was headed to my promised land of peace and joy.

As scary as the thought of starting over as a single mum in a new city was, I was at peace knowing that God had given me a promise: "Fear thou not; for I am with thee: be not dismayed; for I am thy God: I will strengthen thee; yea, I will help thee; yea, I will uphold thee with the right hand of my righteousness" (Isa. 41:10 KJV).

I arrived in Houston, Texas, on February 24, 2014. As we unpacked the truck, I felt like I was breathing the newness of fresh air into my whole body.

My daughter, about one year at the time, could not hold her excitement. She ran from room to room, with her arms spread wide, as the landlord showed us our new home. At times my young daughter would lie down and roll on the floor. I wondered why she was so excited. I wanted to believe she could connect with the feeling of freedom, less anxiety, peace, and quiet.

Shila stayed with us for three days, after which I paid her ticket to fly back to Birmingham, Alabama. I got busy acquiring the necessary documents to set up life in our new city. I could not apply for any job till I received my Texas nursing license, so I applied for it and waited for its arrival. Meanwhile, I changed my driver's license and bought auto insurance. Thankfully, I had paid my rent for two months and bought enough groceries to last us a while. I would need to replenish only the perishables. Eventually I got a job as a supervisor in an assisted living facility, and life started to normalize.

A year later, Shila called. "I'm about to retire, and I want to move from Alabama. But I'm not sure where to go."

She had family who lived in three different states, and I expected her to pick one. But when she said she wanted to move to Houston, I was thrilled. I was excited and offered her to stay at my place till she could figure things out. It was the least I could do for all the kindness she had shown me and my daughter when I was desperate for help.

Once she'd retired from her job, she put her furniture and other possessions into storage in Alabama, flew to her home in Africa for a few weeks, then arrived in Houston with only her clothes. She had given her car to one of her daughters. So, without a car, it became quite a challenge for her to get a job. I worked Monday through Friday, morning to evening. That left no time for me to drive her around for a job search. Meanwhile, I was ok to provide both shelter and food for her as she waited to settle down.

CHAPTER 15

A FRIEND'S BETRAYAL

In August of 2015, my daughter and I traveled to Kenya for one month to see my family. Shila stayed in my apartment and used my car while I was gone. I had paid ahead all my bills, including rent, before I left because without a job, Shila wouldn't be able to cover these expenses. Two weeks before I returned home to Houston, she called and said she had received some money from her retirement benefits and was about to travel back to her home country in Africa. She would return a month later.

I arrived back to the United States the first week of September. I learned that Shila had received a check of over $15,000 before she left. To my surprise, the electric bill of $75 was overdue and the power was about to be disconnected. I struggled to understand how she left with all that money and never thought of paying the light bill, especially considering that I was taking care of everything else in the house. I had helped pay bills when I stayed at her house. As I thought about it, it wasn't my place to decide how she spent her money. I let it go.

A month later, she was back from Africa and showed up at my place. Broke! She still had no car, no phone, no job, and no place to live. Yet she blew all that money on God knows what.

I felt used and misused when she gave me an attitude because I could not call off work and drive her around.

At times I had her drive me to work, then she used my car to look for a job. I didn't mind helping her this way, but she wasn't grateful and, in fact, made remarks about how she expected better treatment than I was giving her. Sometimes when I asked her a question, and she ignored me for no good reason. I wasn't sure what I needed to do to please her. I bent over backward, but it was never enough for her.

One evening, as I headed to work an extra shift, I received a call from Rex. I had previously blocked his number. I wondered how and why he called after so long a time had passed.

"I'm returning your call," he said.

"But I didn't call you," I said.

He insisted that I had.

"Hold on." I checked my phone call history and, sure enough, I found an outgoing call to him. I thought back to a time when Shila had used my phone to call her daughter. She had obviously also called Rex. I was confused as to why she had called him. I demanded to know what they had discussed. I didn't feel safe considering that she was staying with me.

"She asked me for money . . . again. I'm tired of her calling me all the time, asking for money."

"Money for what?" I was shocked that she'd been going to him for money.

"She's helping watch my family." He said

My heart sank! Is that why she chose to come to my place, to watch me and my daughter for you? How long have the two of you been at it behind my back? He could not stand the heat of the questions I threw at him, so he hung up.

I had never felt so betrayed! How could the person I trusted so much do this to me? How was she comfortable transacting with my enemy? I had been feeding her, providing accommodation, and the man who had abused me had been paying her to spy on me!

It's hard to believe the level of evil in people's hearts. Truly, some of the most poisonous people come disguised as friends and family.

Who on earth could I trust?

I confronted Shila when I got home. "Why are communicating with Rex, and working for him, when you know all that has transpired between us?"

She fidgeted and wrung her hands. "I'm sorry. Rex had asked me to try to bring you two back together."

My mouth dropped open. Shila used to say that I deserved better than what I had with Rex. She had encouraged me to move on, assuring me that I would find a better husband than Rex. All the while taking money from him with a promise that she would bring us back together!

No wonder she was against any relationship I tried to start. I had moved miles away from my abuser only for someone who called herself a friend to report back to him about my life. Truly, how much money was our lives worth?

Was that the reason she chose to live with me instead of her family members? Because she was on a mission? How safe was I if the person whom I had trusted with my life was a spy? I totally agreed with whoever said that it's better the enemy who slaps you in the face than a friend who stabs you in the back!

At that moment I again woke up to reality. Relationship with Shila was toxic. I began to reflect on prior events that had seemed rather odd at the time, but I had put it out of my mind. For example, she had allowed Rex to bring gifts while I was still at her place. She had encouraged me to accept them. When I recalled her knowing Rex had burned me that tragic day, goose bumps erupted on my flesh. How had she known that? I hadn't mentioned him. How could someone be so accurate on something that had happened in their absence? Now, with clear hindsight, I saw Shila in true light. Though I had no way to prove anything I speculated, fear and suspicion filled me. I was scared that she had given Rex my home address, my work address, and all the other details of my life that he could use to get to me.

I had to escape this trap. But Shila still depended on me for everything, and I couldn't just throw her out. Thankfully, she got a job as a live-in caregiver, and a friend sold her an old car he wasn't using. However, my relief was short-lived.

Even with her having a job and transportation, she returned to my apartment on the weekends. The guy I was dating, who knew everything that was happening, suggested that I should tell her I was moving in with him. It was meant to discourage her from coming back, and she would not know where I was staying. It worked well, and she found a place to stay when she was off work.

Two weeks later she called. "Why did you lie to me? I drove by your place and saw your car parked outside."

Rather than answer her, I had my own question. "Why did you come looking for me?"

"I just wanted to make sure you moved."

"Why? Why would you do something like that?" I kept putting her "accusation" back on her.

Finally, she had no answer but only stuttered some nonsense excuse.

After we hung up, I decided to tell her the truth. I didn't want to speak with her so I texted her that I loved her and appreciated her friendship, but I was no longer comfortable with the fact that she was acting like glue, connecting my past that I was trying to forget to the future I was busy creating. I wrote that her actions were putting both my daughter and me at risk by being untrustworthy. She didn't reply to the text, and, to date, that was the last time I heard from her.

Strangely, after I sent that text, I got several calls from Rex, who had acquired a new phone number. He called several times a day. I ignored the calls and later blocked the new line, too. He hated that his point of contact was finally disconnected.

One Sunday afternoon, he called from another line and threatened me. "You think Texas is heaven? I can still get you."

Knowing what he was capable of and being aware that he most likely knew my address, I could not take it lightly, so, I reported the threat to the Houston Police Department. They assigned a warrant of arrest should he come to Texas. I notified my lawyer, which resulted in a court hearing. I also received authorization to be released from my lease, which still had four months remaining, and relocated to a new address.

At the hearing, Rex was ordered not to contact me through any means or he would be imprisoned. I'm happy to report that I haven't heard from him since.

This whole journey left me with loads of anger, bitterness and confusion. Why were the people close to me working against me? I wondered if there were any genuine friends anywhere in the world.

CHAPTER 16

FORGIVENESS AND HEALING

To this day, years after Rex's attack and Shila's betrayal, I still wonder how I lived all that time with someone who was clearly capable of doing so much harm. To me, it's like that story in the Bible of Daniel being thrown into a den of lions. Some situations call for divine protection to survive.

Even though his kind of love felt strange from the beginning, the whole time we were having issues. I thought it was normal in every family. But some of the things he said had left me confused. For example, "I would kill for you" if he even suspected another guy's interest in me.

Remarks like this disturbed me, but then I convinced myself, "Well, he is just trying to say he loves me." What I didn't realize was that he was threatening me!

He had a serious issue with insecurity and was very uncomfortable with any male talking to me or looking at me, even his friends. Without my knowledge, he deleted from my contacts list any male friends he was uncomfortable with. I also noted that he wanted to control my money, citing that we were then husband and wife, and as head of the family, he should control all our finances. Since I didn't earn much, he made sure all my money went to paying various bills. That left me with no savings. Looking back, I see by so doing, he was making sure I had no way to escape. Before long, he started advising me about some of my female friends, saying that they had bad reputations. He didn't want me to be seen with them because I was a nice girl. It was easy to believe him, since he had come to America two years before me. I assumed he knew better.

As you can see, he exerted a lot of manipulation and control. Everything he said was supported by evidence. It was subtle, yet real. Before I knew it, he became my best friend and the main source of advice. Knowing that I didn't have anyone to talk to, he started attacking my self-esteem and confidence by suggesting areas of my body that needed improvement. The truth was, I knew these things. I didn't need anyone to point it out, especially not by putting me down. Not long after we had started living together, I became self-conscious. My self-esteem took a downward spiral. I also become somewhat dependent on him. I felt incapable of making major life decisions without his opinion. Little did I know that I was playing into his hands. His control would later escalate to sexual and physical abuse.

As a matter of fact, I never knew I was in an abusive relationship until I was in nursing school, second semester, when my psychology lecturer took us students through the types and signs of abuse. It was then that I learned I had been emotionally abused. Rex ticked all the boxes: isolation, humiliation, threats, intimidation, excluding, and other treatments that diminish one's sense of identity and self-worth.

If any or all of these signs are at work in your relationship, please do not ignore them. Domestic abuse is a monster that hides behind a pretty name. By the time the abuser is finished with you, your self-worth is shattered, leaving only negative thoughts. You feel hopeless and unable to think for yourself. The thought of facing life without your abuser is scary. That is their goal. They make you feel incapable of having a normal life, and they sometimes tell you how no one else could ever love you. This is why it is vital that you work on your self-worth. When a person's self-esteem is healthy, they won't believe the abuser. You can see through his tactics and realize you don't have to put up with it early in the relationship.

Also, if you are in an abusive situation, be very careful with whom you share your experiences/information. Some people don't have integrity, and they might mishandle such delicate information and end up hurting more than helping. When I realized that my marriage was not normal, I shared with two friends, both of whom had experienced abuse in their marriages, thinking they would be in a better position to understand my situation and offer help. But to my surprise, they ended up being a danger to my own life. They told everything I shared with them. Rex aware of everything I was thinking, including my planned escape.

I was tempted to be bitter and resentful because of the betrayal by people I trusted. Then I came across a saying by Nelson Mandela, whom I greatly admire. "Resentment is like drinking poison and then hoping it will kill your enemies." I prayed to God to help me let the hurt of betrayal go. I allowed Him to avenge for me like He promised: "It is mine to avenge; I will repay. In due time their foot will slip; their day of disaster is near and their doom rushes upon them" (Deut. 32:35 NIV).

Looking back now, I have no ill feelings toward Rex or his co-conspirators because, as Joseph said, "You intended to harm me, but God intended it all for good. He brought me to this position, so I could save the lives of many people" (Gen. 50:20 NLT).

Rex pleaded guilty to throwing boiling water on me and was sentenced to ten years in prison. As much as and in the many ways he had hurt me, I felt bad for him. I had been in a self-imposed prison all the while I was married to him. Doing time was difficult. But his actions required consequences. All I needed was freedom from him. My young daughter was not safe in his hands because, given the chance, he would rather get even with me for escaping his trap than be a father.

My daughter's safety depended on the quality of my decisions. But I didn't have the knowledge to make the best ones. I needed divine wisdom on how to make decisions from that point on.

There were all sorts of voices from friends, foes, and in between as to what I should do with Rex regarding his guilty verdict. Some said I should let him rot in prison. Others thought it was wise to forgive him and reunite for the sake of our daughter, while a few advised me to let him be part of our daughter's life, even if I didn't want him back. The more the noise that flooded my head, the more confused I got. I asked the Lord to guide me.

When Rex and his lawyer begged my lawyer and me to drop the charges, his lawyer said that Rex was ready to do anything, including sign off the rights to his daughter in exchange for no prison time. Hearing that, I felt peace in my heart. I knew that was what God wanted me to do. Besides, Rex already was bound to a restraining order that he was to stay away from us for years. I agreed, and he instead of going to jail, he did four years of probation.

Taking that option meant my daughter would grow up without knowing her biological father, but it was much better that growing up in fear of what her father would do to her or her mother. I pray that one day he will take heed of the issues residing deep inside of him and take necessary steps toward the healing process. Only then will he be able to live a normal life and have a normal, meaningful relationship with anyone. I also believe that God in His wisdom will make sense of the whole thing someday.

When I had moved to Houston, Texas, I was set to start living life on my terms. I loved my newfound freedom. Surprisingly, I wasn't scared that everything was new. I hooked up with a friend who was a divorced single mom. She seemed to have moved on, and I aspired to do the same. She loved to have fun. I have never been a party girl before, but I enjoyed having a few drinks, dancing, and mingling with other friends, both male and female. It was through her that I met a guy who became my boyfriend. I didn't care to even think about marriage, so the first condition after confirming that he was single was that we could just have fun, nothing serious and definitely no marriage! Turned out that's what he wanted as well.

He was from West Africa, Muslim by religion, which was perfectly fine with me. I didn't need anyone who spoke the same language, shared the same religion, or had any kind of similarity as my abuser. All I wanted was to catch up on the fun I had missed.

He was and still is a great guy. He and my daughter totally clicked. He was patient enough to listen to my complaints of how I was abused over and over again, without being mean or judgmental to me. He was very positive and affirming, and he also believed in me, which helped me build up my wounded self-esteem much faster. At the time, I attended Lakewood Church on Wednesdays, since I worked on weekends, and listened to a lot of pastor Joel Osteen sermons on YouTube. What I didn't know then was that his messages were the therapy I needed to heal the emotional wounds of my past.

Two years into the relationship, just when I was starting to get comfortable, he told me his family, who lived in the United States, was pushing him to marry. At first, I thought he was joking, because we had established a clear boundary not to marry. A month after telling me of his family's desire, I found out that they had invited a woman over from Africa. She was staying in his house. Part of me was very disappointed, because I had grown to love him, but I was not ready for such a serious commitment.

His leaving my life made me realize that I had to look for another man to fill his shoes. I got busy window shopping for a man. It was hard to find someone who could replace him and fit into the person I had become. I was tempted to call him back to keep me company, but he had gotten married. I had to respect it. I had so much time on my hands, and I didn't know how to spend it.

One day, I heard Bishop T.D. Jakes preach. He said that everyone should go to God and find out why they were created. Apparently, I had a purpose on earth, but I didn't know it. I decided to search for my purpose.

Around that time, a friend introduced me to her church, Faith City, in Katy, Texas. I visited and learned that their mission was "Connecting you to God, so you can live a renewed life, discover your purpose and change the world." Clearly, God had led me to this church. It was then that I decided to totally commit my life to Christ. I chose to follow that decision quickly and seriously before I made another huge mistake. I got baptized and became a committed member of the church. I must say, that was the best and the most important decision of my life. God dealt with the remaining issues of bitterness, anger, and insecurities that had been holding me down. He has been renewing my mind ever since. I am a different person. Truly, finding God is finding love.

Having no boyfriend forced me to channel my energy and attention to God and His love for me. I decided to put aside the dating business and focus on loving myself the right and healthy way and finding my purpose. I also needed to give my daughter all the love and undivided attention she deserved.

Sometimes, life is hard. Raising a child single-handedly is never easy, but we haven't lacked anything. I have learned to totally depend on God's Word and His promises. He is our provider. I am confident that the same God who protected me when I didn't know I was in danger will keep us safe for the rest of our lives.

FINAL THOUGHTS

If you don't know who you are, your value and self-worth, chances are you will be used, misused, and even abused. Predators prey on those who suffer identity issues. Your identity, however, can only come from your Maker. He is the only One who holds your reason for being. God says in Jeremiah 1:5 that He knew you before He placed you in your mother's womb and set you apart for a specific purpose.

The Bible also tells us, "But you are a chosen race, a royal priesthood, a holy nation, a people for His own possession, that you may proclaim the excellences of Him who called you out of darkness into His marvelous light" (1 Pet. 2:9).

We have been made kings and queens by believing in the Lord Jesus to declare God's excellent work on earth, not to be abused. By understanding that we are royalty, every one of us should carry ourselves with dignity, not allowing treatment that does not befit us. We set the standards of how people love and treat us. No one will love or treat us better than we do ourselves. When we let someone abuse us, we have lowered our personal standards and given others the power to do whatever they please. Whenever you feel like you are being treated with anything less than the value you have placed on yourself, seek and use wisdom, and vacate the situation as soon as possible.

Being married, single, or divorced does not add to or subtract from your value. The true measure of who you are is determined by God through His word. When you acknowledge that God made you for a purpose, you will focus on Him as He begins to unfold the reason for your being.

Also, get to know people well, their background and their family traditions, before you get involved with them. Listen to your instincts, which is Holy Spirit giving you guidance for your life. Disobeying your instincts will eventually have consequences. I believe I would have had a totally different outcome if I had immediately obeyed the instinct that told me to leave the relationship. God knows what's best for your life. He also knows our innermost desires. He knew Rex's motives were not good and was trying to save me from years of frustration. I paid dearly for my disobedience. My goal in sharing this is to save you from making the same mistakes I did and to encourage you to choose wisely.

I have discovered that the ultimate love, the one I missed all my life, is the love of God, who loved me enough to make me, to breathe His breath into me, and, most important, to give His only Son to die for me. The truth is, I was looking for love in all the wrong places; hence, I found myself in a near-death situation. I didn't know my value, and my abuser exploited me as a result!

But now I know and believe that I'm a masterpiece, made in an amazing way for God's glory.

I believe everyone should focus on finding their purpose for life before they look for a mate. In my opinion, many marriages are failing today because we are operating out of divine order. We settle with someone and then later begin the process to discover our purpose. Too often we realize we've chosen the wrong partner for the work we were created to do. So, we either settle in a frustrated marriage and forsake our purpose or quit the marriage and pursue our purpose. Both choices are painful. We should start looking for destiny helpers instead of life partners.

Why Do We Stay in Abusive Marriages?

Why did you stay in the marriage if you knew you were being abused? I get asked this question the most. Honestly, I don't have a definite answer. But I believe I stayed as long as I did because I had some issues as well. I had low self-esteem. I did not quite believe in myself, and I cared too much about what people would think or say if I got out of the marriage.

When you are secure in who you are, you won't care what anyone says about you. You make decisions based on who you believe you are and what you want in life. Because I didn't correctly value, love, and respect myself, I allowed someone to devalue, disrespect, and walk all over me in the name of so-called love. One big reason many people remain stuck in toxic and abusive relationships and friendships is that they fear if they leave, someone will judge them.

People with low self-esteem too easily fall victim to abusers. Their need for validation is a big foothold for the abuser to manipulate. They take advantage of people who don't fully believe in themselves; they become a crutch for their unsuspecting prey. As soon as they become dependent, the abuser exerts control through a variety of dirty tricks to keep them hooked, fully disarming them of what little self-esteem they may have had. They lose themselves and their power. This is when the abuser can do or say anything, and they have no choice but to take it. If this describes you in any way, please seek help immediately. (See Resources section.)

Most single people are busy looking for a mate. It is of utmost importance that you are aware of the kind of individuals who are out there; the number of emotionally and mentally disturbed men and women out to trap their next victims. Once they get you into their cold arms, your life will never be the same. Not only will they destabilize your life, but your children's, too, if you have any.

The repercussions of staying in those marriages are usually great on children. Your remaining in the relationship hurts their futures as well as yours. That is the plan of the enemy, but you can, and must, break out of it. For with God, all things are possible. I believe if you call on Him, He will hear and answer you!

RESOURCES

The National Domestic Violence Hotline

Active Beat: "10 Telling Signs You're Trapped in an Abusive Relationship"

Healthy Place: "Leaving an Abusive Relationship: Why Can't I Just Leave?"

Made in the USA
Columbia, SC
30 January 2025

52961243R00067